The World's Harvest

BEVERAGES

Jacqueline Dineen

ENSLOW PUBLISHERS, INC.
Bloy St & Ramsey Ave.
Box 777
Hillside, N.J. 07205

story of how tea, coffee, cocoa, fruits, and grains are grown, manufactured into drinks, and distributed all over the world.

Contents

The picture above shows bottles of soft drinks going through a shrink-wrapping machine.
[cover] The cover picture shows a line of tea-pluckers on a plantation in north-eastern India.
[title page] The picture on the title page shows Ghanaian cocoa farmers cutting open the harvested pods to remove the seeds.
[1–25] All other pictures are identified by number in the text.

This series was developed for a worldwide market.

First American Edition, 1988
© Copyright 1985 Young Library Ltd
All rights reserved.
No part of this book may be reproduced by any means without the written permission of the publisher.

Printed in the United States of America

10 9 8 7 6 5 4 3 2 1

LIBRARY OF CONGRESS
Library of Congress Cataloging-in-Publication Data

Dineen, Jacqueline.
    Beverages / Jacqueline Dineen.
      p.   cm. -- (The world's harvest)
    Includes index.
    Summary: Explains how tea, coffee, cocoa, fruits, and grains are grown, manufactured into drinks, and distributed all over the world.
    ISBN 0-89490-210-5
    1. Beverages--Juvenile literature. [1. Beverages.]   I. Title.
II. Series: Dineen, Jacqueline. World's harvest.
TP505.D56 1988
663--dc19
                                                              88-1183
                                                                CIP
                                                                 AC

Introduction

When you enjoy a cup of tea or coffee or chocolate, or open a can of fizzy drink, do you ever wonder where these drinks come from and how they are made? Each type of beverage has a fascinating story behind it, and in this book I am going to tell you about them.

First I tell you how tea is grown in countries like China, India and Sri Lanka. The tea bushes are grown in hundreds of thousands on the plantations, and when the leaves are ready they are picked and dried and prepared for

[1]

making the drink we know. The lady in picture [1] is a tea picker in India. I explain why there are so many different types of tea, how they are blended together, and what the job of the tea taster is.

In chapter 2 we look at how coffee is grown and harvested. I tell you how the coffee farmers pick the fruits which contain the beans, and how the beans are taken out of the fruits. Then I explain how coffee gets its flavour by roasting the beans, and how it is sold.

In chapter 3 we visit a cocoa farm to see how cocoa is produced. Cocoa beans grow in big pods on the cocoa tree and these pods are cut off the tree by hand. I tell you how the beans are scooped out of the pods and fermented to bring out the chocolate flavour. Then I explain how the cocoa beans are made into the cocoa we drink.

Soft drinks also come from ingredients which grow in the soil. Most soft drinks have fruit in them. Some have spices, like ginger. In chapter 4 I explain how these drinks are made, and how the bubbles are put into sparkling (or 'fizzy') drinks.

In the last chapter I tell you a bit about alcoholic drinks like wine, beer and spirits. Wine is made from grapes growing in a vineyard. Beer is produced from malted cereals. Stronger drinks like whisky and gin are made by an interesting process called distillation.

It is fascinating to think about the exotic countries and foreign workers, the harvesting under the tropical sun, the packing and canning and bottling plants, all involved just to get that refreshing beverage into your mouth.

All the beverages I describe in this book go through a process called 'fermentation', which is almost impossible to explain! Briefly, it is a chemical change which causes a kind of decomposition. Some substances automatically start to ferment if there is moisture and the right amount of heat. Other substances ferment only if an already-fermenting substance is mixed with them. Fermentation causes substances to change, for example it changes sugar into alcohol.

1 · *Tea*

When you make a cup of tea, you pour boiling
water on to the leaves of the tea bush. Tea
bushes grow in tropical or semi-tropical parts
of the world, where there is plenty of hot sun
and heavy rain. The largest tea producer is
India. Picture [2] shows an Indian tea estate
with the bushes stretching into the distance.
The oldest, and in some ways most famous,
tea-growing country is China. Indian teas have
a strong flavour, while China teas are usually
more delicate and fragrant in taste.

[2]

Other main tea-producing countries are Sri Lanka, Kenya, Malawi, Tanzania, Mozambique, Zimbabwe, Indonesia, Japan, Taiwan, and Bangladesh. No tea is grown in Britain, but the British like to drink it. Almost 25 per cent of all the tea produced in the world is bought by Britain!

The tea bush is an evergreen plant which grows at any altitude up to 2,100 metres (7,000 feet). The best quality tea is produced at the higher altitudes, though the plants grow more slowly there.

The bushes are grown from seed, or from cuttings taken from other bushes. It takes between three and five years for a plant to grow into a bush which is suitable for tea production.

Plucking the leaves

When the bushes are ready, the leaves are picked. This is called plucking. The bush is not stripped of leaves. Only the youngest leaves can be used for tea, so the pluckers just pick the tip of each shoot—the leaf bud and two top leaves of each branch.

During the growing season new leaves quickly appear, so the bushes are plucked every 7–14 days. As this work has to be done by hand, a tea estate needs hundreds or even thousands of pluckers. Tea plucking is a skilled job because the workers have to judge which leaves to pick and which to leave alone so that the bushes will stay healthy. If the bushes were left to grow naturally they would produce only a few, very high, branches, and there would not be many young leaves to take. Therefore

the bushes are pruned into a spreading shape, [3]
with a flat top called a 'plucking table'. This
shape gives more branches with young leaves.
The bushes are pruned often so that new leaves
keep growing.

The tea pluckers are often women, and in
India they make a colourful picture as they go
amongst the low, green bushes in their
brightly-coloured saris. As you can see in the
pictures on the cover and on page 3, they carry
large, wicker baskets on their backs for holding
the shoots they pick. When a basket is full, the
plucker takes it to a collection point. You can
see a collection point in picture [3]. This is
where the tea is checked and weighed. A
skilled plucker who can work quickly picks as
much as 35 kilogrammes of leaves in a day.
This amount makes 9 kilogrammes of tea,
which will provide almost 3,600 cups.

The tea factory

[5]

[4]

When the leaves have been plucked and weighed, they are taken to the factory on the tea estate. Here, they are made into black tea or green tea. Black tea is made by fermenting the leaves. The leaves for green tea are left unfermented.

Most of the tea we drink every day is black tea. The leaves for black tea are spread on racks and withered (dried) in currents of warm air. Then the withered leaves are crushed to release the natural juices. This part of the process is called 'rolling' because the traditional method was to roll and twist the leaf. Nowadays, though, the leaves are cut or minced by machine, and you can see this being done in picture [4].

Juices are squeezed out of the leaves during crushing, and the leaves are then left in a damp atmosphere. This causes the leaves to ferment (see page 4 for an explanation of this). The leaves you see in picture [5] are still green but as they absorb oxygen from the air they will change from green to a bright copper colour. After a period of 2–4 hours, the leaves are passed through a hot air dryer to stop the fermentation. By this time, the tea has turned black and now smells like the tea we know.

During the processing, the tea leaves have been broken up into pieces of various sizes. The tea is now sorted into grades by sieving machines. Tea with large, whole leaves is called Leaf Tea. The next grade is Broken Tea, which has large broken leaves. Fannings is the grade found in ordinary packet tea, and Dust is the type put into tea bags.

Green tea is made in a slightly different way.

Before rolling, the leaves are scalded or
steamed so that they will not ferment. The tea
is then made in the same way as black tea.
Green tea is not so popular in most countries
as black tea because it has a slightly bitter
taste.

[6]

Did you know that there are 1,500 different
types of tea? But a tea bush is a tea bush, so
why are there all these flavours? Well, all sorts
of things affect the flavour. The height at
which the bushes are grown makes a difference.
So does the climate. So does the type of soil.
The way the bushes are cultivated, and the
method of plucking and drying the leaves, all
affect the flavour of the tea.

The tea is now ready to leave the tea estate. Have you seen those big, square plywood boxes which are often used by removal men to pack crockery and other small articles when moving house? Well, picture [6] shows what they were originally made for. Two factory workers are lining the boxes with foil and filling them with tea. It will be sold to a tea blending company, where it will be prepared for the shops. Countries which import tea have their own tea blending companies, so the tea chests may have thousands of miles to travel by sea.

Tea is sold by brokers at an auction, either in the country where it was grown or in the country which is buying it. Tea auctions work like this. The tea producer has a selling broker who sells the tea for him. The blending company which is buying the tea has a buying broker. Both sides have tea tasters, who taste samples of the tea that is for sale.

It is fascinating to watch the tea tasters at work. Picture [7] shows the lines of samples, and the bowls in front of each from which the taster samples the brew.

The tea blending company mixes different teas together to create all the flavours you can buy in the shops. The packet of tea you buy may contain thirty different sorts! The tea blenders taste samples from each chest they have bought, and decide how they are going to mix the tea. The recipe for the blend is then sent to the factory where the teas are mixed.

The blended tea is put into packets or boxes or tea bags. Then the tea is ready to leave the factory for its journey to the shop and supermarket shelves.

A broker is a person employed to buy or sell goods for someone else, without ever owning them.

[7]

2 · Coffee

Coffee is made from roasted and ground coffee beans. Coffee beans are not vegetables. The coffee tree bears fruit called cherries, and the beans are the seeds found inside the fruit.

The coffee tree is a tropical, evergreen shrub which grows naturally to three or four times the height of a man. In cultivation, however, it is usually pruned to a pyramid shape no taller than 3.5 metres (10 feet). Its delicate white flowers look like orange blossom and smell like jasmine. Picture [8] shows flowers and cherries together on the branch. Coffee grows in Central and South America, Africa and Asia.

The best known coffee country is Brazil, but it is produced in fifty countries, most of which are in the tropics. Coffee needs a warm climate and plenty of rain, but frost kills it. It is an important crop—people in nearly every country drink it, and it provides employment for about 20 million people.

Brazil has huge plantations with thousands of trees growing on them. However, a lot of the world's coffee is grown on small farms. On these farms much of the work is done by hand, as it has been for years.

Coffee seeds are planted in nursery beds so that they can be watched over until they are about a year old. Then they are transferred to the fields. They will not bear fruit until three or five years have passed, but they have to be carefully looked after all the time. The trees need pruning and spraying against pests and

[8]

disease. The ground must be fertilized and kept moist and free from weeds. Coffee trees do not like too much direct sunlight, so taller trees are sometimes planted round about to provide shade.

After all this hard work, the tree is at last ready to produce blossom and cherries. At first the cherries are green, then they ripen from yellow to a deep red and look rather like the cherries on a cherry tree.

Harvesting the cherries

In Brazil the climate ripens all the cherries together, and they are harvested by machine. In other countries they ripen at different times, and you often get red and green cherries together on the same branch. The workers have to go between the rows of trees, picking the fruit by hand and putting it into baskets slung over their shoulders. The worker in picture [9] is picking the few red ones, and leaving the green ones to ripen.

In some countries the fruit is left on the trees until it is so ripe that it falls to the ground, or can be shaken off the branches.

Coffee trees blossom and produce fruit three or four times a year, so the harvesting season is a long one. The picking can go on for five or six months. Even so, a coffee tree produces only about 2,000 cherries a year. That sounds a lot until you realize that it takes 4,000 cherries to make 1 kilogramme of roasted coffee!

Many of the small farms are worked by a single family. Everyone is kept hard at work, gathering fruit and tending the trees. The

[10]

larger plantations in countries like Brazil need to employ hundreds of workers to harvest the fruit.

When the coffee has been harvested, the pulp of the fruit is removed from the bean. This can be done by the 'wet' method or the 'dry' method. The wet method needs expensive machinery and is used mainly on the larger plantations. Small farms (if they have a dry climate) rely on the dry method, though some send the cherries to a co-operative for processing.

This is how the wet method works. A pulping machine removes the pulp from the cherries as soon as they have been picked, while they are still fresh and moist. This leaves the bean surrounded by a protective coating called parchment. To loosen this parchment, the beans are soaked and fermented in tanks, as you can see in picture [10]. Then they are washed thoroughly and dried, either in drying machines or by laying them in the sun for a while. The last stage is to 'hull' the beans in a machine, which removes the parchment and polishes the beans.

The dry method is much simpler. Picture [11] shows freshly picked cherries being left there to dry. After two or three weeks the pulp is dry enough to be removed with the parchment in the hulling machines.

Roasting the beans

If you were to boil up some green coffee beans and drink the liquid, you would be very disappointed by the result. Green beans do not taste of anything much. Coffee has to be roasted to bring out the flavour. This should be done as late as possible before it is brewed into a drink, so the coffee is exported in its raw, green state. It is sold to manufacturing companies, and it is they who will do the roasting.

However, small samples are roasted and tasted before the coffee is shipped abroad, because it has to be graded for quality. This is the job of the coffee taster who you can see in picture [12]. He roasts a sample from each farm, grinds the beans, and makes small cups of coffee. He smells a sample—is the aroma right? Then he tastes it and carefully considers the flavour. His opinion is important, because the coffee manufacturing companies rely on it. As with tea, there are many different coffee flavours, and the coffee taster has to give an accurate description of all the beans he tries.

[11]

[12]   The coffee manufacturing companies buy green beans of various flavours. After roasting them they sell them as whole beans, as ground coffee, or as instant coffee.

The beans are roasted until they turn from green to dark brown. Roasting times and temperatures are varied to make different flavoured coffee. Longer, hotter roasting gives a darker, stronger coffee.

Instant coffee is convenient because it dissolves in water straight away, whereas ordinary ground coffee takes time to brew. Only the soluble part of the bean is used to make instant coffee. The rest—the 'grounds' you find in a pot of fresh coffee—is discarded. Instant coffee is made by spray-drying or freeze-drying coffee powder or granules. It does not have such a strong flavour as freshly ground coffee beans but it is popular because it is so quick to make.

Coffee is now one of the world's largest industries. In the United States, for example, almost 150 billion cups are drunk each year. That's a lot of coffee!

3 · Cocoa

All cocoa and chocolate products come from cocoa beans, which grow in pods on the cocoa tree.

The cocoa tree grows wild only in the tropical rain forests of South America. However, it is also cultivated in West Africa and other parts of the world where the climate is similar to its native environment. About 40 per cent of the world's cocoa is grown in the West African countries of Ivory Coast and Ghana. The trees are also cultivated in other countries, including Mexico, Brazil, Nigeria, Equador, San Domingo, Sri Lanka, and the West Indies. Altogether, more than $1\frac{1}{2}$ million tonnes of cocoa is produced each year.

[13]

The wild cocoa tree is quite small, but the cultivated varieties can grow up to eight metres in height. The cocoa fruit, which you can see in picture [13], is over twenty centimetres long. It has a thick husk, and contains about forty seeds (called beans). Each tree bears between twenty and thirty pods a year.

The cocoa farms may be large plantations owned by cocoa companies, or small plots of land worked by a farmer and his family. As more than half the world's cocoa is grown in West Africa, I will tell you about life on a cocoa farm there.

Cocoa trees like warmth, moisture, and some shade. If a farmer decides to start a cocoa farm, he must first clear a patch of forest to provide the right sort of place for the trees to grow. He cuts down trees, shrubs and creepers, but he leaves some of the taller trees to provide shade for the cocoa trees. He grows his cocoa plants among other crops for the same reason. Banana trees and other crops can shade the young cocoa plants, as well as provide food for the family.

A nursery bed is a place where young trees or other plants are raised from seed, before being transplanted elsewhere.

The cocoa seeds are planted in nursery beds and transferred to the crop fields when they are between two and three months old. As the plants grow the farmer keeps them free from pests and disease, fertilizes the soil, and removes any weeds.

The cocoa trees start to bear fruit called pods when they are four or five years old. The pods ripen from green to a rich yellow or orange. Not all the pods on a tree ripen at the same time, so they have to be picked individually. In picture [14] the lower ones are being cut off the tree with a cutlass, but the farmer in picture [15] has to fix a curved knife to a long pole to reach the pods growing high on the tree.

Harvesting and fermenting

The farmer and his workers go round the trees several times during the harvesting season, so that they can pick the pods when they are at their best. If they pick them before they are ripe, or leave them till they fall off the trees, the beans inside will not make such good cocoa.

As the pods are gathered, they are taken to a collection point on the farm. On the title page of this book you can see the pods being opened with a cutlass to remove the seeds. The seeds and pulp are scooped out and laid in a heap on a layer of banana or plantain leaves.

I have already explained how tea and coffee have to be treated to bring out the flavour. Cocoa is no different. Raw beans taste bitter and they have to be fermented to bring out the smell and taste of chocolate.

The heaps of beans are covered with more leaves and left for nearly a week in the sun. The temperature in the heap rises, causing the beans to ferment and to change colour from purple to brown. The heap of beans is turned from time to time so that air can circulate and the beans are fermented evenly.

[14]

When fermentation has finished, the wet beans are put into baskets and carried to the farmer's house. In picture [16] you can see them spread out on mats of split bamboo cane and left to dry. The mats are on stakes so that any liquid and bits of dust can fall through on to the ground. At night, and when it rains, the farmer rolls up the mats to keep the beans dry.

[15]

After four or five days the beans are dry enough to be sold. The farmer puts the beans into large sacks and takes them to his local buying agent.

[16]

The agent works for the Government. He examines samples of beans from each sack to make sure they are of good quality for export. Then he weighs the beans and pays the farmer for them. The agent buys cocoa from all the cocoa farmers in the area. He mixes beans from different farms to get the quality he wants.

Although cocoa grows only in hot climates, chocolate does not keep well in the heat.

[17]

Therefore cocoa is exported in its raw state to the cooler countries, and made up into chocolate and cocoa powder there. Picture [17] shows sacks of beans being loaded on to ships.

Processing into cocoa powder and chocolate

When the cocoa beans arrive in the country which is buying them, they are taken to a cocoa factory. They are roasted to loosen the shells and to give the cocoa its chocolatey taste and smell.

Next, the beans are crushed between rollers to crack the shells into small pieces. The bits of shell are blown away, leaving behind the edible part called the nib.

It is from these nibs that cocoa and chocolate are made. The nibs contain about 55 per cent cocoa butter. This cocoa butter is too rich for cocoa, so the nibs are ground up into a thick chocolate liquid and about half the cocoa butter is removed. The remaining cocoa and cocoa butter is cooled, and solidifies into a solid block. This block is then ground into powder to make cocoa for drinking. The left-over cocoa butter is used in making the chocolate we eat as bars or in sweets.

4 · Soft drinks

A 'soft' drink is a drink which is not alcoholic or intoxicant. It usually means a drink made of fruit juices, or a mixture of fruit juice with water, sugar, and flavourings. We drink them to quench our thirst, and because they taste nicer than water!

There are two sorts of water used in soft drinks—still, and sparkling. Still water is the stuff which comes out of the tap. Sparkling water has bubbles in it, which make your mouth tingle, and get up your nose. The bubbles used to come from gases found in some spring water. Nowadays it is made by pumping carbon dioxide into still water. Sparkling drinks are often called fizzy drinks.

There are three main types of flavoured soft drink—fruit juices, concentrated drinks, and sparkling (fizzy) drinks. I shall describe each one briefly.

An intoxicating liquor (or drug, etc.) is one which lessens control over physical and mental powers. In small doses it gives a sense of well-being. In large or prolonged doses it can lead to insensibility, poisoning, and death.

[18]

Fruit juices

Fruit juices are normally made in the country where the fruit is grown. They are made by crushing the fruit in machines, to squeeze out the juice. The most popular fruits for this purpose are oranges, pineapples, grapefruits, tomatoes (yes, a tomato is a fruit!), and apples. Picture [18] shows apples being crushed in a press. The main producers are the United States, Brazil, Israel, Spain, and Sicily. Italy exports a lot of tomato juice. Britain makes

21

apple juice and blackcurrant juice. These fruit juices are usually kept pure with nothing added, though some preservative may be added to keep them fresh for longer.

Fruit juices are not particularly thirst-quenching, and are usually drunk in a small quantity before a meal as an appetizer.

Concentrated drinks are those which have had most of the natural water taken out of them before being bottled. They therefore need to be diluted with water again before they can be drunk. Many fruit juices can be concentrated. Orange, lemon, blackcurrant, and barley water are some of the favourite concentrated drinks. Picture [19] shows a lemonade production line.

After the juice has been squeezed out of the fruit, and the oil has been squeezed out of the peel, the juice is concentrated to about six times its natural strength.

Sugar and preservatives are added. Sugar is a basic ingredient of all soft drinks except pure fruit juices. Sugar comes from cane or beet, and in picture [20] you can see cane being cut in the West Indies.

Acids (or acidulants, as they are called) are put in to give the drink a sharp, refreshing flavour. The acidulants found in soft drinks are citric acid from citrus fruits, tartaric acid from grapes, and malic acid from apples.

Concentrated drinks

Concentrating a liquid means increasing its strength by reducing the proportion of water.

[20]

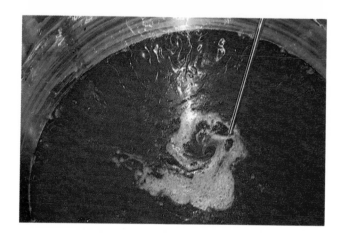

[21]

Sparkling drinks include lemonade, cola, tonic water, soda water, and ginger beer. They are made either from concentrated juice, or from 'comminuted' fruit. Comminuted fruit means that the whole fruit has been crushed and some of the pulp removed afterwards. Comminuted fruits also have sugar, preservatives, and acidulants added.

In the syrup room at the soft drinks factory, the fruit preparation is mixed with the sugar and other ingredients in stainless steel tanks. How many of you recognize the mixture in picture [21]? It then passes to the filling room where the bottles or cans are waiting. The filling machine has a syruper, which measures out the right amount of syrup into each container.

At this stage the preparation has been the same whether the drink is to be a concentrated or a sparkling drink. Now, for sparkling drinks, carbonated water is added to the syrup. Carbonated water is made by forcing carbon dioxide into water, under pressure, in a machine called a carbonator. Picture [22] shows empty bottles going into the machinery, and full ones coming out on the other side.

Concentrated drinks have a small amount of water put into them. However, the taste of water is affected by the area it comes from. Therefore the water is filtered first, to get rid of any chalk or other substances.

The filled bottles are carried on a conveyor belt to the 'capping heads'. Here, caps or screw tops are put on. Then the bottles go through the labelling machines, and they are ready to leave the factory.

People certainly like soft drinks. In the United States, sparkling drinks are much more popular than concentrated drinks, and each person on average drinks 182 litres of sparkling drinks each year. In western Europe about 15,000 million litres of sparkling drinks are sold each year. [22]

5 · *Alcoholic drinks*

Alcohol is a liquid produced by the fermentation of sugar. It is usually prepared by treating grain with malt and adding yeast. It also forms naturally, for example on grapes decomposing in the sun. It is the intoxicating part of fermented beverages.

Alcohol has many important uses, and the making of alcoholic drinks is only one of them. People drink alcoholic beverages because they make them 'feel good', as well as because they have an agreeable taste.

There are three main types of alcoholic drink—wine, beer, and spirits.

Wine

Wine can be made from all sorts of fruit and vegetables. People who make wine at home use elderberries, rhubarb, blackberries, even parsnips. But most wine is made from grapes.

Grapes grow in bunches on vines. The vines are supported on stakes or wire, and they are regularly pruned so that they grow no taller than a man can reach. They need a warm, sunny climate with moderate rainfall. They will not grow in very cold countries, or in the tropics where it is too hot and humid. Countries which produce wine include France, Italy, Germany, Spain, Greece, the United States (mainly in California) and southern Australia. In picture [23] vineyard workers are tending the vines on a hillside in France.

White wines are normally made from white grapes, and red wine from black grapes. There are hundreds of varieties of grape. The winemaker chooses the one which will grow best in the soil and climate of his vineyard.

The vines have to be looked after very

carefully. They must not get too cold or too
wet. They must be kept free from diseases and
pests, and the grapes must be harvested at just
the right time.

   The grapes are picked in the autumn. Some
winemakers use mechanical harvesters to pick
the grapes as quickly as possible. Others have
to rely on picking the fruit by hand, and hire
workers just for the season—some vineyards
need several hundred pickers.

   The harvested grapes are crushed in
machines called 'presses', which separate the
juice from the skins and pulp. The grape juice
is put into a large vat, and yeast is added to
make the mixture begin fermenting.

[23]

When fermentation has finished, the wine is carefully transferred to a new vat so that most of the solid bits are left behind. The wine stays in the new vat until all the sediment has settled to the bottom. It is then poured into another vat, or into a wooden cask, and left to 'mature' for several months.

'Maturing' is a rather mysterious process of ageing, caused by the wine absorbing oxygen through the porous wooden walls of the cask.

All this activity takes place on the vineyard. Many vineyards also have their own bottling plants, but others send the barrels of wine to be bottled elsewhere. If the wine is to go abroad, it is transported all the way in barrels, and is bottled in the country which buys it.

Most wine is drunk as an accompaniment to meals. The most famous wine of all— champagne—is traditionally drunk at celebrations such as weddings.

Beer

Beer is a refreshing drink made from barley (and occasionally other cereal grains). It has less alcohol than wine, and can therefore be drunk to quench thirst as well as for its enjoyably bitter taste.

The barley is first turned into malt, which is germinated barley. It is steeped in water, then spread out in a warm and moist atmosphere until each grain begins to put out a shoot and grow. At the right moment, germination is stopped by heating it gently in a kiln.

The malt is then lightly crushed and mixed with other cereals and hot water in a vessel called a 'mash tun' which you see in picture [24]. This process converts the starch in the grain into sugar, which will ferment when yeast is added.

The 'sweet wort' is transferred to a copper where it is boiled with hops. Hops are the dried cones of the hop vine, and give the beer its bitter flavour which is what beer-drinkers like. The wort is cooled, and yeast is added to make it ferment. Fermentation takes several more days. The wort has now been converted into beer—but it is not yet ready to drink. This 'green beer' is allowed to ferment for a second time. This produces more carbon dioxide which is absorbed into the beer and, as you already know, it is carbon dioxide which causes the fizziness in all sparkling drinks.

Any solids still left in the beer are cleared by adding 'finings'. These small particles sink to the bottom, pulling any solids with them.

[24]

Sweet wort is the name of the liquid drawn off the mash of malted grain.

Now the beer is sent in wooden barrels, or in metal kegs like those in picture [25] to hotels, public houses, clubhouses and similar places. Or it is first put into bottles or cans and sold in those places, or in shops and supermarkets.

Spirits

Spirits are never drunk to quench thirst, but for the sake of their taste. They may be drunk in only very small amounts because they have much more alcohol in them than wines or beers. The best known spirits are whisky, gin, vodka, brandy, and rum.

The extra alcohol in spirits is produced by a process called 'distillation', and I will tell you how it works. Alcohol boils at a lower temperature than water. So if you heat beer or wine, which has a lot of water but only a little alcohol, it is the alcohol which boils first.

The alcohol turns to vapour as it boils, and this vapour can be collected. When cooled it turns back into a liquid which is strong alcohol.

Whisky is made from some kind of grain. Scotch whisky is made from malted barley. American whisky is made from rye, maize, malted barley, or malted rye. Canadian whisky is made from rye. The grains are fermented with yeast in the same way as for beer, before the liquor is distilled. Vodka, also, is made from grain.

The other spirits are made from various ingredients. Gin is made from juniper berries. Rum is made from sugar cane molasses. Brandy is made from distilled wine.

All the beverages in this book, alcoholic and
non-alcoholic, are a valuable part of the
world's harvest. They provide a livelihood to
millions of people in every part of the world.
They provide sustenance for *hundreds* of
millions. All the ingredients—tea, coffee, cocoa,
fruit, cereal grains, sugar, yeast—come from
the soil.

There is just one more ingredient which does
not come from the soil, and that is water.
Water is an essential part of every beverage. I
have not talked much about water here. It is
such a big subject that I have written a
separate book about it, which you will find in
the 'World's Harvest' series.

The last ingredient

Index

Acknowledgements for photographs: The Brewers' Society, nos. 24, 25; H. P. Bulmer Ltd, no. 18; Co-op, no. 19; French Tourist Office, no. 23; International Coffee Organization, nos. 8, 9, 10, 11, 12; Paul Nash, picture on title verso and nos. 21, 22; Rowntree Mackintosh, picture on title page and nos. 13, 14, 15, 16, 17; Tate & Lyle, no. 20; The Tea Council, cover picture and nos. 1, 2, 3, 4, 5, 6, 7.